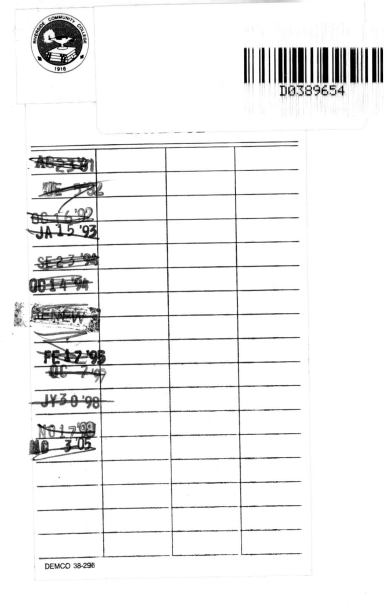

How to Simply Cut Hair

A step by step guide to the six basic
haircuts that can be combined or altered
to create just about any hairstyle.

Written and illustrated by

Laurie Punches

Published by Punches Productions
South Lake Tahoe, California

Punches, Laurie C.
How to Simply Cut Hair
"A Punches Productions Book."

Publisher's cataloging in Publication Data
1. Haircutting. I. Punches, Laurie.
1. Title

1 2 3 4 5 6 7 8 9 10

Library of Congress Catalog Number
88-92443

ISBN 0-929833-06-3

To make haircutting an easier and more enjoyable experience... **we have made the following teaching aids available to you.** Just fill out and send in the order form located in the back of this book. For prompt delivery dial 1-(800)/833-8778 to order.

A HAIRCUTTING KIT $29.95

Professional 5" ice-tempered haircutting scissors, a plastic haircutting cape, a 7" plastic all-purpose comb marked in inches, a neck duster brush, a spray bottle and five plastic butterfly clamps packed in a nylon duffle bag for convenient storage.

HOW TO SIMPLY... VIDEOS

"How to Simply Cut Hair"	**$29.95**
"How to Simply Cut Children's Hair"	**$29.95**
"How to Simply Perm Hair"	**$19.95**
"How to Simply Highlight Hair"	**$19.95**

These instructional videos follow the same step by step instructions found in the books.

HOW TO SIMPLY.... BOOKS

"How to Simply Cut Hair" (beginners haircutting)	**$8.95**
"How to Simply Cut Hair Even Better" (advanced haircutting)	**$9.95**
"How to Simply Cut Children's Hair"	**$7.95**
"How to Simply Perm Hair"	**$6.95**
"How to Simply Highlight Hair"	**$6.95**

A PRACTICE DOLL HEAD $24.95

This manikin head and holder has 19" long human hair. It attaches to just about any table, desk or counter top providing hours of haircutting practice... **at your own pace!**

ACKNOWLEDGEMENTS

The author would like to acknowledge the help and support of Jack Rogers and Mark Rayburn for layout, design and production, Debbie Rogers, Rod Ruple and Carla Martinez for editing, Steve Björkman for the cover illustration, Virgil Masalta for the author's photograph and my sister Emma, for the hours spent caring for our children during the many hours devoted to writing and illustrating this book. Thank you very much.

DEDICATION

This book is dedicated to my husband, companion, and best friend Pete Oster, and our four beautiful children Ryan, Katie, Michael and Jeffrey.   I love you.

DISCLAIMER

This book in no way claims to be a substitute for beauty school. It is merely a haircutting guide for the non-professional to be used in the home. The word "client" simply refers to the person who's hair is being cut. No professionalism is inferred.

TABLE OF CONTENTS

Foreword

Introduction

1 The Tools

2 The Shop Set-up

3 To Start

4 Handywork

5 Bangs

6 Creating the Outline

7 Cut 1 The All One Length Cut

8 Cut 2 The Undercut

9 Cut 3 The Beveled Cut

10 Cut 4 The Long Layered

11 Cut 5 The Medium Layered Cut

12 Cut 6 The Short Layered Cut

13 Alterations

14 Combinations

15 Ways to Wear Hair

16 Styling Tips

Conclusion

FOREWORD

Even if you have no knowledge or experience cutting hair, this book can teach you how to cut just about anyone's hair. This step by step haircutting guide can be used for all types of hair whether long, short, thick, fine, straight or curly. Fashions and styles will keep on changing, but basic haircutting always stays the same.

This book teaches the six basic haircuts. Haircutting for men and women is identical, the only variables being length and angles.

An instructional video that follows these same steps, along with **other teaching aids** can be ordered by using the form found in the back of this book.

INTRODUCTION

Four ingredients are needed to successfully cut hair. The first ingredient is to have a strong **desire to learn.** This desire may be to save money by stretching the time between haircuts, cut family and friend's hair or just for fun.

The second ingredient is to have **a knowledge of haircutting** which this book will provide.

The third ingredient is to gain **confidence** which comes naturally with understanding basic haircutting. Confidence grows with experience.

The forth ingredient is to **risk** - each of the six basic haircuts taught in this book. Soon you will become familiar with each of the six basic haircuts and be combining and altering them to create various styles. For example, the same haircut can be changed by parting the hair on either side, or down the middle. It can be combed forward or pulled back off the face, sculpted, gelled, blow dried or left natural. Sideburns can be left long, medium, short, angled, straight or softly rounded. Perming and highlighting can give hair the personality and texture needed for achieving the look you want.

Before starting the haircutting process, you will need to take a realistic look at the person's hair you are about to cut. This person will be addressed as the "client" throughout the remainder of this book. The client will be referred to in the feminine gender throughout this book with the exception of the section on shorter haircuts where the masculine gender will be used.

Communication

Take the time to discuss what hair style your client wants. The most common complaint I've heard is, "She didn't cut my hair the way I wanted it cut."

Communication is the key to successful haircutting. Take the time to listen to what your client wants in a hairstyle. Repeat what you heard her say. Do this until you have a clear picture of your client's desired hairstyle crystalized in your mind. Some helpful questions to ask might be how much length do you want taken off? Do you like a part? If so where? Do you want bangs? If so how much? How long? Do you like wearing your hair forward or back off your face? Do you want a clean blunt line to your cut or a soft wispy look? How much ear do you want exposed?

If your client needs your help on deciding what hairstyle would be best suited for her type of hair, consider the head and facial shape as well as her hair texture.

Head and facial shapes

In helping your client choose her hair style, you want to choose a cut that will give her face the appearance of being perfectly oval. This can be done by adding width to a narrower face and adding height to a wider face. To give the appearance of more width, use medium to long bangs with chin length hair or shorter. Longer layers also give the illusion of having thick, full ends which makes the narrower face appear wider.

Height can be added by cutting short layers at the crown. Either very short hair or shoulder length and longer will enhance the wider face. Never draw attention to the areas of width by having the finished length end at the point of greatest width. This will only emphasize the width that you are trying to camouflage. You want to draw attention to other areas to minimize the appearance of width.

Types of hair

There are many textures and types of hair: thick, medium, thin, curly, wavy, straight, coarse, medium and fine. Most hair can be cut by simply following the directions in this book. Here are a few helpful suggestions for problems you might encounter.

Straight, fine hair

When you cut straight, fine hair, choppy cutting lines are often left in the hair. Tiny, steep, triangle shaped slivers can be cut into the very ends of your client's hair to break up these harsh lines. This method is shown in the chapter, "Alterations".

Curly hair

Curly hair has the tendency to shrink when it is dry. The tighter the curl, the more shrinkage will result when the hair is dry. To compensate for this loss in length, leave the hair a little bit longer than you think you'll need.

Thick hair

Sometimes when cutting thick or coarse hair you will find your scissors unable to cut through the thickness easily. Take the hair down in sections to accommodate the amount of hair instead of trying to cut it all at one time. This method is shown in the chapter, "Creating the Outline".

Wavy hair

Wavy hair is the easiest and most forgiving hair to cut. The soft, natural curvature will hide most slight imperfections. Just follow the directions.

A QUICK OVERVIEW

Now you are ready to start cutting hair. Begin by reading the entire book from beginning to end. This will familiarize you with the six basic haircuts.

Before beginning each haircut you will read and follow the directions for: The Tools, The Shop Set-Up, To Start, Handywork, Bangs, and Creating the Outline.

Choose from the six basic haircuts the one that most closely defines your client's desired hairstyle. If none of these are quite right, you can create your own style by combining and/or altering one or more of the six basic haircuts.

A blowdryer and curling iron can be used to style the finished haircut.

The purpose of this book is to teach the art of haircutting not to just memorize haircuts. If you combine the knowledge you learn from this book with experience and your own creativity, you will be soon able to cut just about anyone's hair with confidence.

1

THE TOOLS

Being sure you have all of the necessary tools is the **first step** for each haircut.

In order to cut hair well, you will need a small assortment of tools. This ensemble consists of a pair of ice-tempered, stainless steel, haircutting scissors, a plastic all-purpose comb marked in inches, a water-proof cape, a spray bottle, a neck brush and five plastic or metal hair clips. **You can order an inexpensive quality kit containing these tools by filling out the order form at the back of this book and placing your order**. Another place these tools may be individually pur-chased is at your local beauty or barber sup-ply. A small investment in quality tools will make haircutting a much more enjoyable learning experience.

Scissors

A pair of 5 inch, ice-tempered, stainless steel, haircutting scissors with a finger tang. This is the most important tool for haircut-ting.

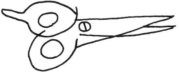

Comb

A 7 inch, plastic comb marked in inches for the purpose of measuring and comparing hair lengths throughout the cut.

Cape

A large piece of waterproof material that fastens at the back of the neck to protect your client from pieces of cut hair.

Mister

A plastic spray bottle used to keep the hair wet throughout the haircut.

Neck Duster

This is used to remove pieces of cut hair that tend to cling to your client's face, neck and clothes. It will lessen the possibility of itching and discomfort that can be caused by these hairs.

Clamps or Clips

5 plastic butterfly clamps or 5 long, thin, metal clips will help keep unwanted hair up and out of the way.

(Extra optional tools)

Apron

A piece of water resistant material that fastens at the neck and waist. It is used to protect the stylist from pieces of cut hair as well as chemicals such as perm solution, bleach, peroxide and tint.

Razor

An electric or battery operated shaving razor with a trimming edge. This can be used to remove excess neck, side burn and moustache hair. There is an alternative method using scissors, taught in the chapter "Alterations".

Thinning shears

These are shears used to take out unwanted bulk and thickness in the hair. An alternative method of thinning hair using scissors is also taught in the chapter, "Alterations".

Blowdryer and curling iron

A blow dryer and curling iron are the tools usually used to dry and style your finished haircut.

2

THE SHOP SET-UP

Setting up shop is the **second step**.

You don't need to spend too much time and energy worrying about where to set up shop. Just about any place will do. I've cut hair in almost every room in the house.

The bathroom seems to lend itself well to haircutting. A large mirror, good lighting, an easy to clean floor, and a convenient counter top where tools can easily be reached makes haircutting an easier and much more enjoyable experience.

3

TO START

Preparing your client's hair for the haircut is the **third step** in haircutting.

BRUSH

Start by thoroughly brushing the hair. This will loosen any dry scalp flakes and bring the natural oils from the scalp to the ends. The bristles will help to massage the scalp and stimulate good blood circulation as well as eliminate snarls.

SHAMPOO

After a good brushing, always start by shampooing the hair. This will make the hair more manageable and pliable while cutting.

Apply a small amount of shampoo, massage well and rinse until the hair is free of suds. Repeat if needed.

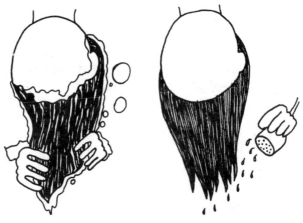

CONDITION

A conditioner may be applied if the hair is dry or full of tangles. Squeeze a moderate amount of conditioner in the palm of your hand, rub your hands together and distribute it evenly to the hair shafts.

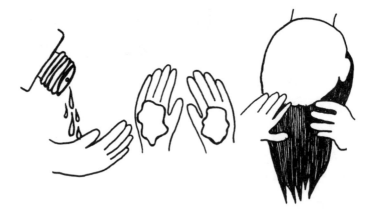

Now rinse the hair and towel dry.

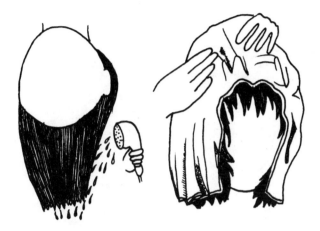

4

HANDYWORK

Learning to hold and manipulate the scissors and comb is the **forth step** in haircutting.

Feeling comfortable with 'handywork' comes with practice. At first it may seem awkward, but don't get discouraged... soon it will be second nature. Be sure to take the time to read and practice this "handy work" before going any further.

HOLDING THE SCISSORS

Begin by placing the thumb of your more dexterous hand through the large hole and your ring finger through the small hole of the scissors. Rest your pinky on the finger tang. The scissors will stay in this hand while the comb will continually change hands.

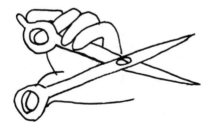

HOLDING THE COMB

Slip just your thumb from the large scissor hole. Now lay your scissors in the palm of your hand.

Place the comb in that same hand (now holding the scissors) between the index finger and thumb. Now comb the hair using the wide tooth end of the comb.

With your free hand, grasp the hair, between the index and middle fingers. Slide your fingers down the hair shafts applying just enough pressure to create tension. Fingers should stop sliding just above the point at which the hair will be cut.

THE COMB EXCHANGE

While still holding the hair between the index and middle fingers of your less dexterous hand, place the comb in that same hand between the thumb and index finger.

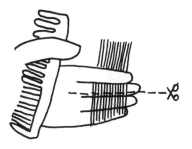

CUTTING THE HAIR

Place the thumb of your more dexterous hand back through the large hole of the scissors. You will cut the hair just beneath the index and middle fingers holding the hair. Use these fingers as a straight edge and cut parallel to them.

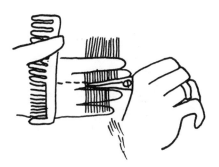

5

BANGS

Cutting the bangs is the **fifth step**. (If bangs are not necessary skip over this chapter.) There are three types of bangs: **light, medium** and **heavy,** from sheer to full bangs.

To create bangs you will use a semi-circle part which extends from one temple to the other. A shallow semi-circle will create light bangs, a deeper one will create fuller bangs.

Decide what type of bangs you want...

| Light | Medium | Heavy |

and part the hair in a semi-circle accordingly.

Top View

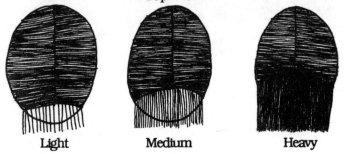

| Light | Medium | Heavy |

This parting will separate the bang hair from the rest of the hair. Comb the remaining hair away from your client's face and clip it up and out of the way. This will help define the bang section. Comb the bang hair directly forward, laying the wet hair flat against your client's forehead so that it sticks to the skin.

Decide upon the length and the contour of the bangs.

Do you want a soft curved line... or a straight blunt line?

Straight   Curved

Use the distance between the bridge and the tip of your client's nose as a measuring tape. Cutting closer to the bridge creates shorter bangs while cutting closer to the tip creates longer bangs.

Short   Medium   Long

Remember wet hair will shrink when it is

dry, so when in doubt leave length. **It just takes a few minutes to cut more length, but growing hair takes time.**

Start cutting wet, flattened bangs at one temple moving toward the center and ending at the other temple.

Cut the entire bang section to the desired amount, length and curve.

If no layering is desired, the bangs are finished. If layers are desired go on.

Layered bangs are softer and fuller than blunt, or unlayered bangs. This is because the bangs have less weight. Layers are a result of the hair being elevated while being cut. The higher the hair is elevated the more layers will result.

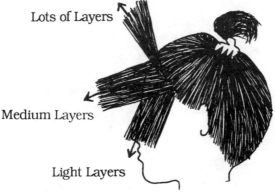

Choose from the following pictures how

much layering is wanted.

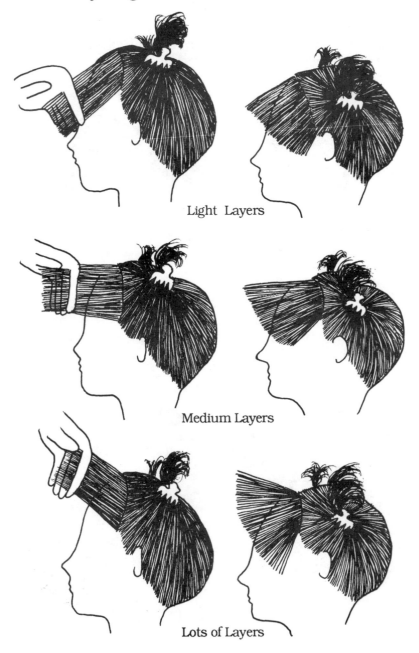

Light Layers

Medium Layers

Lots of Layers

Take the bang section between the index and middle fingers of your less dexterous hand. Pull the hair up to the desired horizontal angle indicated for the amount (little, medium or lots) of layering wanted.

(This chapter shows medium layered bangs.)

Hold the hair tautly at this angle while sliding your fingers down the hair shafts.

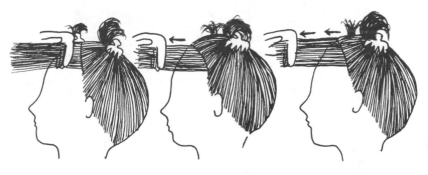

Keep sliding until the underneath hairs begin to fall from your fingers (on to your client's forehead).

Still holding the hair at the same angle, cut the bangs parallel to your fingers.

Now that the bangs have been cut, you may begin "Creating the Outline".

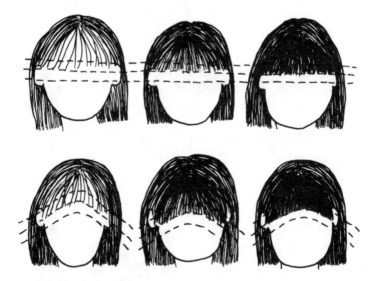

6

CREATING THE OUTLINE

"Creating the outline" is the **sixth step** for all haircuts in this book <u>except</u> the "All one length" cut (where an outline is not needed).

"Creating the Outline" is the foundation upon which the rest of the haircuts are built. It defines the shape and outline of the entire cut. The hair will be cut around your client's face, neck and ears to the varied lengths needed to outline your individual haircut.

Read and follow the directions in chapters 1-5. Hair should be washed and lightly towel dried. If bangs are desired they should be cut before beginning the outline. No part is needed for the outline. Be sure the head is held erect and facing forward to insure symmetry.

Use the crown as a pivot point. Comb the hair down from the crown laying the wet hair flat so it sticks to her face, neck and ears.

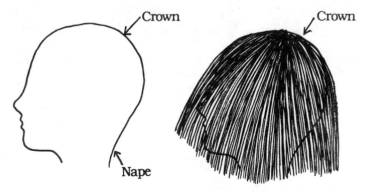

From the following pictures choose the outline that most closely defines the haircut your client wants. (Outline 5 is shown in this chapter.)

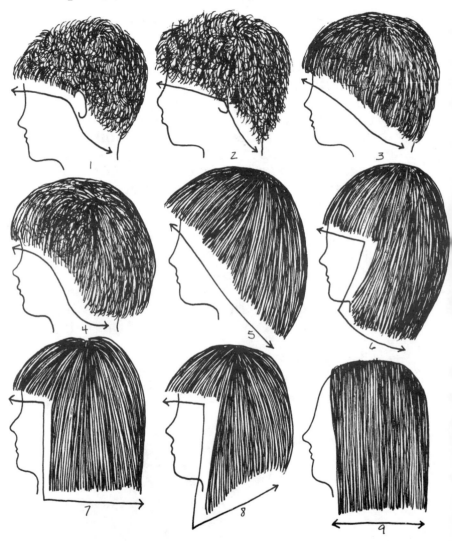

Stand in front of your client. Notice that you can see the shorter 'cut bang' hair length through the long hairs laying over them. Cut these long hairs to the same length and curve as the cut bangs beneath.

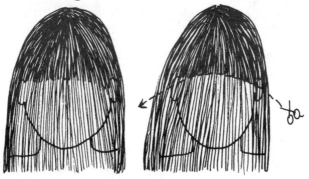

Begin on your client's left, move toward the center and end on her right.

Stand in back of your client. Ask her to show you with her hand the exact length that she would like her hair in the back to be cut.

Cut a 2" wide section of nape hair directly at the center back of her head to the desired length.

Often when cutting thick or coarse hair you will find your scissors unable to easily cut through the thickness. Take the hair down in sections to accommodate the amount of hair instead of trying to cut it all at one time.

You will complete this outline by connecting both the front and back cut lengths. This can be done by cutting both sides of your client's hair.

Stand in front of your client. Begin on her right side. Use the bang length as a guide for cutting the hair laying on top of and beside it. Cut the hair from the front to the back cut section. The side hairs should be cut to the lengths necessary to create the your outline.

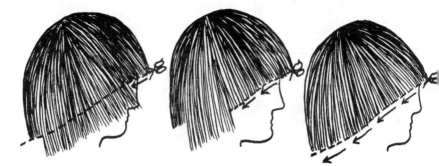

When cutting hair <u>over</u> the ears, take care not to nip the ear. Press the ear flat against your client's head with your less dexterous hand while cutting.

If you are cutting hair <u>around</u> the ears, press each ear forward with your less dexterous hand while cutting the hair.

Stand in back of your client and cut the hair in back of her head.

Now stand and cut the hair on your client's left side, cutting from back to front.

The hair should be cut to the necessary lengths to create the outline of your individual cut.

When the entire outline has been cut make sure your client's head is erect and facing forward. To check if both sides of your cut are identical, stand directly in front of your client at eye level. Take a pinch of hair from the same place on both sides and pull them tautly to compare lengths.

If you are unsure by feel you can also use the measurements on the comb to help compare lengths.

If evening is needed, cut just a little length at a time from the longer side until both sides are even.

Comb your client's hair straight down from the crown with the **wide tooth end** of the comb. Cut any uneven hairs.

Now comb her hair straight down from the crown using the **fine tooth end** of the comb. Cut stray or uneven hairs.

You are now ready to begin the haircut of your choice.

7

CUT 1

THE "ALL ONE LENGTH" OR BLUNT CUT

The first haircut is called the all-one-length cut. Since all the hair is cut to the same length the ends form a straight blunt edge.

Review chapters 1-5. (No outline is needed for this haircut.) The hair should be freshly washed and lightly towel dried. Remember, if bangs are wanted they need to be cut first.

Part your client's hair where she desires. If no part is wanted, part her hair down the middle to create symmetry.

Be sure your client's head is held erect and facing forward throughout the haircut. This will insure symmetry.

Comb your client's hair straight down using the wide tooth end of the comb.

Cut a few strands in the very front of your client's left side to the desired length. (Remember wet hair will shrink when it is dry.)

Now do the same with a few strands from the very front of your client's right side so that the cut lengths on both sides match.

Check to be sure that both sides are even by standing directly in front of your client at eye level. Take a pinch of cut hair from both sides and pull them tautly to see if both sides are the same length.

If evening is needed, cut off just a little length at a time from the longer side until both sides are even and at the desired length.

These cut hairs will serve as a guide for length throughout the rest of the haircut.

To complete this haircut you want to connect both of the cut side lengths by cutting the back.

Start by using the cut hair on your client's right side as a guide to match the hair laying beside it in length. Using your handy work comb the hair on your client's right side of the head straight down.

Cut the hair beside the pre-cut hair to the identical length. Remember to keep your client's head straight forward and erect throughout the cut.

Sometimes when cutting thick or coarse hair you will find your scissors unable to cut through the thickness easily. Take the hair down in sections to accommodate the amount of hair instead of trying to cut it all at one time.

Stand in back of your client. Cut the hair in back of her head from her right to her left.

Now move slightly to your client's left. Repeat the last step **(written in bold)**, moving slowly from your client's right side to her left side until you meet the pre-cut strands of hair on her left.

All the hair should now be the same length.

To check the haircut, be sure your client's head is erect and facing forward. Comb the hair straight down using the **wide tooth end** of the comb. Cut any uneven hairs to create a clean, sharp line.

To double check the haircut comb the hair straight down with the **fine tooth end** of the comb. Cut any stray hairs you might have missed to sharpen the blunt edge.

Now the all-one-length haircut is finished and the hair ready to be styled.

8

CUT 2

THE UNDERCUT

This haircut is often referred to as "the bob" or "page boy" cut. The underneath hairs are cut to a shorter length than the top or surface hairs. This graduation from shorter to longer lengths will cause the ends of the hair to softly curl under toward the face. This particular haircut will take some work on your client's part to respond to your gently pushing her head and neck in different positions.

Read and follow the directions for chapters 1-6 before beginning this haircut. The hair should be freshly washed and lightly towel dried. The bangs should be cut and the outline created before beginning this haircut.

To create the shorter underneath hair length, stand in back and push your client's head completely forward until her chin rests on her collar bone. Comb the hair with the wide tooth end of the comb laying it flat against the back of her head and bent neck so that it sticks to the skin. Using the flat side of your less dexterous hand, flatten your client's hair against her neck.

You will notice that the nape hairs underneath are slightly longer than the surface hairs. Cut the underneath hair in back to the identical length of the surface hair.

Stand on your client's right side and press her head all the way to her left side until her left ear is resting on her left shoulder. Comb and press the wet hair flat against the right side of your client's face and neck so that the hair sticks to the skin. Again you will notice that the underneath hairs are a bit longer than the surface hairs. Continue to cut the underneath hair on her right side to the same length as the top or surface hair.

Stand on your client's left side and press your client's head all the way to her right side until her right ear is resting on her right shoulder. Comb and press the wet hair flat against the left side of your client's face and neck so that it sticks to the skin. Cut the longer underneath hair to the exact length as the surface hair on the left side. (After cutting the entire head of hair, check to be sure no hairs have been missed.)

To check this haircut, roll the head slowly from your client's right, then forward and to her left constantly combing the hair flat against the head and neck with the fine tooth end of the comb. Cut off any long or uneven stray hairs...

so that all of the hair has been undercut.

Now the undercut is finished and the hair ready to be styled.

9

CUT 3

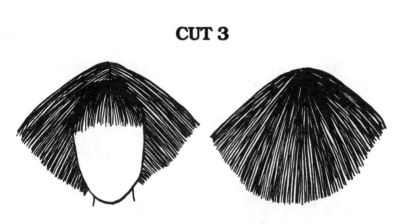

THE BEVELED CUT

The beveled cut is a slightly layered haircut. Layers are a result of the hair being elevated while being cut. The ends have less weight which creates a softer and fuller effect.

Read and follow the directions for chapters 1-6. The hair should be freshly washed and lightly towel dried. The bangs should already be cut and the outline created before beginning this haircut.

Study the pictures below and decide how much layering your client desires for her hairstyle. This will determine at what angle or elevation the hair should be held while being cut. The higher the hair is elevated, the more layering will result. (Medium layers are shown in this chapter.)

Light Layers

Medium Layers

Lots of Layers

Stand on your client's right side. Your client's head should be held erect and facing straight forward. Take a small (approximately 2 1/2" wide) section of hair between the index and middle fingers of your less dexterous hand.

Holding the hair at that elevation, slowly slide the fingers down the hair shafts until the underneath hairs begin to lightly fall from your fingers. (The underneath hairs that have fallen do not need to be cut. Their length has already been established while creating the outline.)

Stop sliding at this point. You will cut the longer surface hair at the point at which you can see the "already cut" shorter lengths beneath. The ends will appear to be a bit thinner. Cut the hair in a parallel line just be neath your fingers using them as a straight edge. Let the section of hair fall from your fingers.

Move slightly to your client's left. Use the cut hair as a guide for length. Take a small (approximately 1" wide) amount of "just cut" hair along with a small (approximately 2" wide) amount of uncut hair beside it. Hold the section of hair tautly between the index and middle fingers of your less dexterous hand at the exact same angle as you held the last section.

Holding the hair at the same angle as last time, slide your fingers down the hair shafts until the underneath hairs begin to fall from

your grasp. Stop sliding at this point.

Make a horizontal cut in the section of elevated hair just below your index and middle fingers, using them as a straight edge to cut along.

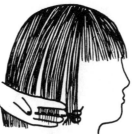

Repeat the steps **(written in bold)**, moving a little to your client's left.

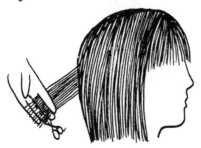

Remember, the higher the hair is elevated,

the more layering will result.

Repeat the same steps **(written in bold)**, moving a little to the client's left each time until the entire head of hair is cut.

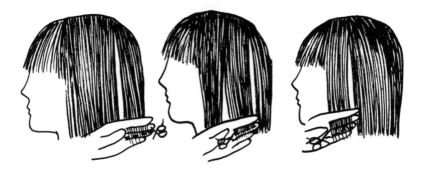

To complete this haircut, take 2 1/2" wide sections of hair and hold them <u>vertically</u> between the index and middle fingers of your less dexterous hand. The ends should form a straight line following the same vertical angle as the arrows in the diagram on page 64 indicate for the amount of layering desired. Cut any stray hairs that stick out from this vertical line.

To check this cut, comb the hair straight down using the **wide tooth end** of the comb. Cut any stray hairs.

Now comb the hair straight down using the **fine tooth end** of the comb and cut any stray hairs.

Now you have completed the beveled cut and the hair is ready to be styled.

10

CUT 4

THE LONG HAIR LAYERED CUT

This hair cut creates lots of layers on top, while leaving most of the weight and length at the bottom. These layers give height and fullness to long hair.

Read and follow directions for chapters 1-6. The hair should be washed and lightly towel dried. The bangs should be cut and the outline created before beginning this haircut.

Hold a few strands of hair from the top of your client's head straight up. Determine exactly how short you want the layers to be on top.

Measure the strands of hair from your client's scalp to your fingers with the measurements on the comb. This will be the determining length at which the layers will be cut.

Stand in front of your client. Have your client stand up and bend forward at the waist. Her head should be totally upside down. Comb her hair directly overhead using the wide tooth end of the comb. Be sure your client's hair is free of tangles and in an orderly fashion in the upside down position.

Hold the comb at the base of the scalp on the

crown. Use the measurements on the comb to indicate exactly where the desired layer length should be cut.

Grasp the entire head of hair at that measured point between the index and middle fingers of your less dexterous hand.

Cut the hair just below these fingers. (The nape hairs do not need to be cut since their length has already been established when you "created the outline".) The closer to the scalp you cut your client's hair, the shorter the layers will be.

Bring your client to the upright position. To check the haircut, comb the hair straight down using the **wide tooth end** of the comb. Cut any long, stray hairs along the outline of the cut.

To double check the cut, comb the hair straight down with the **fine tooth end** of the comb and again cut any stray hairs you might have missed.

The long-layered haircut is finished and the hair ready to be styled.

11

CUT 5

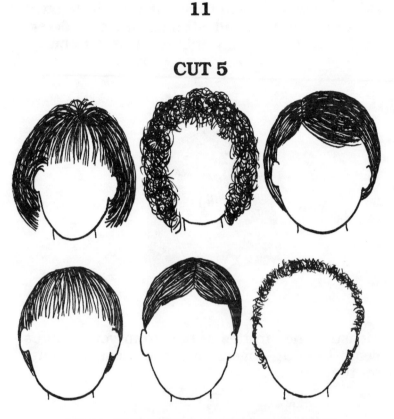

THE MEDIUM LAYERED CUT

The medium layered cut is for a girl's shorter hairstyle or a boy's long to medium length hairstyle. The hair is cut to the same length all over the head.

Read and follow the directions for chapters 1-6. The hair should be freshly washed and lightly towel dried. The bangs should be cut and the outline created before beginning this haircut.

Hold a few strands of hair at the top (crown) of your client's head straight up and determine how short she wants her layers to be.

Measure the strands of hair from your client's scalp to your fingers with the measurements on the comb.

Cut those strands of hair just above your fingers.

This will be the determining length at which the rest of the hair will be cut.

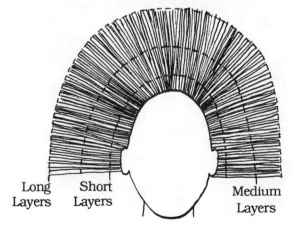

Long Layers   Short Layers   Medium Layers

Picture your client's head as a peeled orange

with all of the sections exposed. Start at the crown and work your way to the nape.

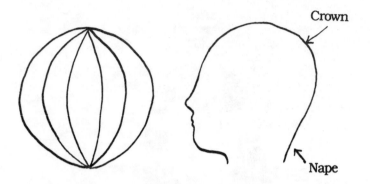

Stand in back of your client. Grasp the crown hairs of the back **orange section** between the index and middle fingers of your less dexterous hand. The fingers should be positioned <u>vertically</u> at the determined layer length.

Cut just above your fingers allowing their contour to be your guide for the cutting line.

Start at the crown and remember to work down the orange section to the nape.

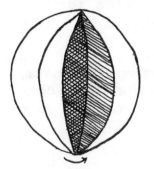

Move to the next "orange section" on your client's right. Clip the rest of the hair out of the way. Start at the crown and work your way to the nape.

Take a small amount of "just cut" hair (approximately 1/2" wide section) along with the new 2" wide section of hair. (The cut hair will serve as a guide for the cutting length.)

Hold this vertical section of hair tautly between the index and middle fingers of your less dexterous hand. The fingers should be positioned vertically at the desired layer length. Cut just above your fingers allowing their contour to be your guide for the cutting line.

Starting at the crown and ending at the nape, cut the rest of the orange section to the chosen layer length. Cut the hair just above your fingers.

Repeat the steps **(written in bold)**, moving slowly from the back section by section all the way to your client's right.

Repeat the same steps **(written in bold)**, moving slowly from the back section by section, all the way to your client's left.

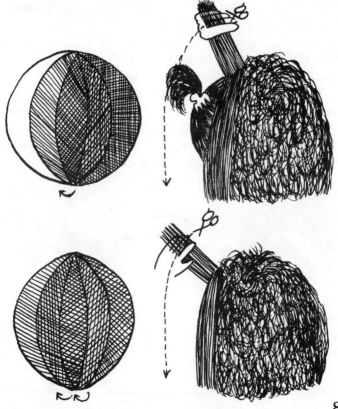

Comb the hair straight down with the **wide tooth end** of the comb. Cut any stray hairs.

Now do the same with the **fine tooth end** of the comb. Cut any stray hairs you may have missed to neaten and define the outline of the cut.

Now check your haircut to be sure every hair is the same length. Picture your client's hair as a corn field. No matter which way you look down the corn rows, (front, side or diagonal) the rows form straight lines. Your client's hair should be the same length all over no matter which direction you pull it.

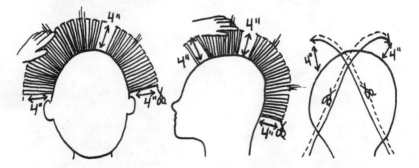

The "medium layered" haircut is now complete and the hair ready to be styled.

12

CUT 6

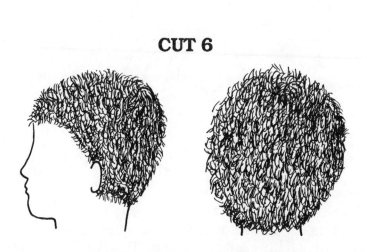

THE SHORT LAYERED CUT

The very short layered cut is often referred to as the shingled or tapered cut. This method can be used just at the nape of the neck, over the ears, or over the entire head. A whole head of hair cut in this method will result in a butch or crew cut. The effect is similar to that of an electric razor cut given at a barber shop.

Read and follow the directions for chapters 1-6. The hair should be freshly washed and lightly towel dried. The bangs should be cut and the outline created before beginning this haircut.

Visualize your client's head as a peeled orange with the sections exposed. Begin at the center **orange section** in the back of your client's head.

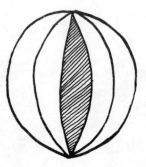

The thickness of the comb will be the determining length at which your client's hair will be cut. The end of the comb with the wider teeth is usually used unless your client wants a shorter length. If this is the case, use the small tooth end of the comb. If a longer length is desired, use your finger depth in place of the comb.

Stand in back of your client. Start with the

back center orange section. Begin at the base of your client's neck with the nape hair. Hold the fine tooth end of the comb with your less dexterous hand laying the wide tooth end flat against your client's neck. The teeth should be facing upward just below his hairline.

Starting at the nape and working toward the crown, slowly move the flattened, wide tooth end of the comb up the center orange section in the back of your client's head. The comb will serve as a rake. Cut the hairs as they stick through between the wide teeth of the flattened comb. The cuts will be made just above the comb so that the thickness of the comb is your guide for length. Work from the bottom to the top of the center orange section in the back of the head until it is completed.

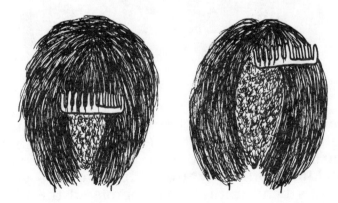

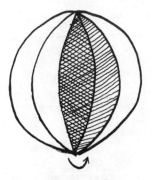

Now move one section to your client's right.

Holding the fine tooth end again place the comb flat against your client's neck with the wide teeth facing upward just below the hairline. Move the comb slowly up this orange section cutting the raked hairs as they stick out between the teeth. Work from the bottom to the top until this orange section is completed.

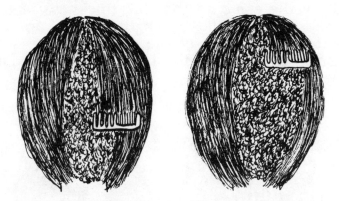

Move section by section toward your client's right. Continue to rake and cut the hair starting at the bottom of each section and working your way up to the top of your client's head until you've completed the right side.

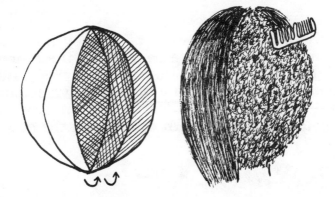

Now do the same procedure starting at the back. Work toward your client's left until the entire left side has been cut.

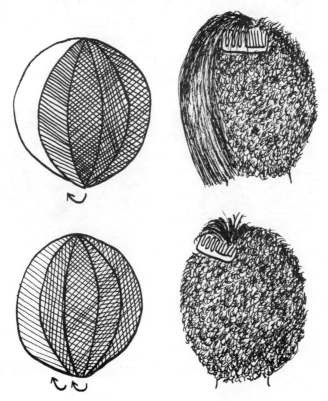

If there are any uneven or choppy lines left behind, comb those areas. Rake the hair in an upward direction from front to back, side to side and diagonally with the wide tooth end of the comb, cut any uneven hairs to create a uniform length throughout the cut.

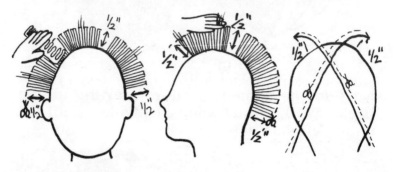

Now the short-layered haircut is finished and the hair ready to be styled.

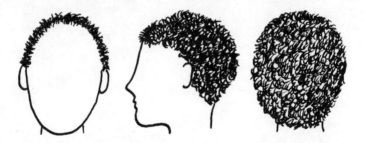

13

ALTERATIONS

Necklines

Use the following pictures to help decide the neckline type your client desires. Begin cutting the neckline hair by starting at one side, working toward the center and ending on the other side. Keep your scissors parallel to the skin to avoid accidentally nipping it.

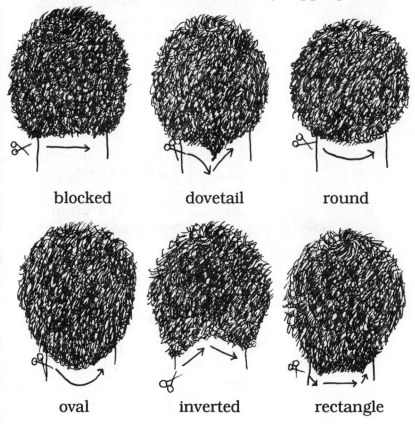

blocked   dovetail   round

oval   inverted   rectangle

Cleaning neck hairs

Lightly scissoring in the neck hairs can give the same appearance as actually shaving the neck hairs. If you don't have an electric razor this method can be used.

Push your client's head all the way forward. This will stretch the skin and give it tension so that there are no folds or creases of loose skin that can accidentally be nipped.

Hold the scissors in your more dexterous hand, laying them flat against your client's neck. Continually glide the scissors open and closed while sliding them along his neck. Always keep the scissors parallel to the neck to keep the tips of the scissors from nipping the skin. Do this until all unsightly neck hairs are gone.

Sideburns

Use the following pictures to decide on the length and angle your client wants his sideburns. Keeping the scissors parallel to the skin, cut the sideburns to the chosen length and angle. Now use a razor to shave the sideburn hair below the cut line for a cleaner look.

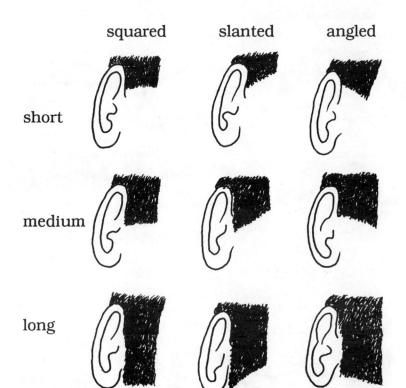

	squared	slanted	angled
short			
medium			
long			

Beards and Moustaches

Use the pictures below to help decide on the style and length of your client's beard and moustache. Always keep the scissors parallel to the skin to avoid nipping the skin. Cut the facial hairs to the desired style and length moving from your client's left toward the middle and ending on his right.

Moustaches

Beards

Cowlicks, Widow's peaks and Whirls

Cowlicks

A cluster of hair that sticks up because of the different directions the hair grows from the scalp. They are often located in the front.

Widow's Peaks

A bunch of hair that forms a peak or V shape. They are usually found at the hairline in front or at the nape of the neck.

Whirls

A group of hair that grows in a circular pattern or spinning wheel fashion. They are usually found in the crown area.

Cowlicks, widow's peaks and whirls can be treated by leaving length. This adds weight to these problem hairs that stick up, so that they lay down.

Breaking up the "Chop lines"

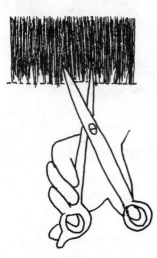

Chop lines are unnatural looking cut marks left by scissors in the hair. They appear most often when cutting straight, fine, blond hair. To camouflage these lines, cut shallow, narrow V shapes into the very ends of the hair These V shapes will break up the harsh, straight edge.

Thinning Hair

There are two ways to thin out unwanted weight or bulk in thick hair. The first way is to use thinning shears. Thinning shears look like a pair of scissors with teeth missing on one or both blades.

These shears are held and used like haircutting scissors. The shears should be held at various angles approximately 3" from your client's scalp. The angle at which the thinning shears are held should constantly change. Thinning should be confined to the bulky areas only and used sparingly so as to avoid creating holes.

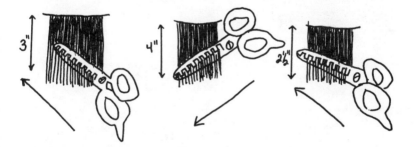

A second way to thin hair (using regular scissors), is to vertically cut deep, narrow V shapes into your client's hair. This can thin out the hair giving it a similar effect as the

thinning shears without having to invest in another tool. Again, thinning should be used in only the bulky or thicker areas to avoid creating holes in your cut.

14

POSSIBLE COMBINATIONS

Combinations is the most exciting and innovative chapter because this is where my teaching ends and your creativity takes over. The only limitation to the millions of hairstyles you can create is your own mind. All of the following hairstyles and more can be done by simply combining two or more of the six basic haircuts and giving them a twist. Even the same haircut can look different by just parting the hair on either side or down the middle, combing it forward or pulling it back off the face. Hair can be sculpted, blowdryed, gelled or left natural.

Each of the illustrated combinations give a front, side and back view of the hairstyle. The combinations are broken down into four categories: outline (chapter 6), bangs (chapter 5), haircut(s) that are combined (each are separate chapters 7-11) and alterations (chapter 13).

Combinations should be attempted **only** after you feel comfortable with each of the six basic haircuts. I hope this chapter encourages curiosity and inspires creativity within you. By simply combining the knowledge found in this book with your own creativity, you can cut just about any hairstyle imaginable.

Outline: 9   **Bangs:** none   **Cuts:** cut 1

Outline: 4   **Bangs:** Medium   **Cuts:** cut 1

Outline: 5   **Bangs:** none   **Cuts:** cut 2

Outline: 5   **Bangs:** Medium   **Cuts:** cut 2

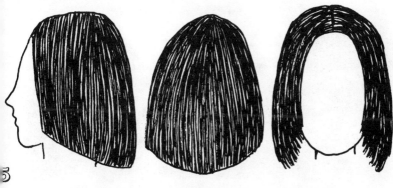

Outline: 8   **Bangs:** none   **Cuts:** cut 2

Outline: 8   **Bangs:** heavy   **Cuts:** cut 2

Outline:7 **Bangs:** medium **Cuts:** cut 2

Outline: 4 **Bangs:** heavy **Cuts:** cut 1

Outline: 1 **Bangs:** heavy **Cuts:** cut 5
Alterations: round neckline, short square sideburns

104

Outline: 8 **Bangs:** medium **Cuts:** cut 2

Outline: 8-right 5-left **Bangs:** none **Cuts:** cut 2

Outline: 8-right 5-left **Bangs:** none **Cuts:** cut 1

105

Outline: 9 **Bangs:** none **Cuts:** cut 1

Outline: 7 **Bangs:** light **Cuts:** cut 1

Outline: 7 **Bangs:** medium **Cuts:** cut 2
(cats-eye shape)

16

Outline:7 **Bangs:** medium   **Cuts:** cut 3-front and sides
                                              cut 2-back

17

Outline: 8 **Bangs:** heavy **Cuts:** cut 1-front, cut 3-sides
                                               cut 2-back

18

Outline: 7 **Bangs:** medium   **Cuts:** cut 4

107

19

Outline: 4 **Bangs:** heavy **Cuts:** cut 3 (slightly beveled)

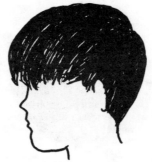

20

Outline: 1 **Bangs:** heavy **Cuts:** cut 5
Alterations: dovetail neckline

21

Outline: 7 **Bangs:** heavy **Cuts:** cut 3

22

Outline: 7 **Bangs:** heavy **Cuts:** cut 4

23

Outline: 2 **Bangs:** heavy **Cuts:** cut 5
Alteratins: dovetail neckline, short slanted sideburns

24

Outline: 7 **Bangs:** medium **Cuts:** cut 3

25

Outline: 2-lower nape   **Bangs:** none   **Cuts:** cut 6-nape,
Outline 8 rest   cut 5-sides
                                                                 cut 2-(rest)

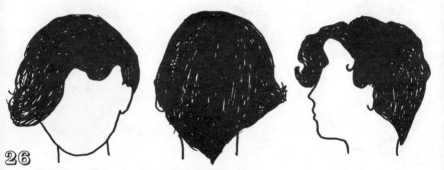

26

Outline: 5-right 7-left **Bangs:** none **Cuts:** cut 3
Alterations: dovetail neckline   (slightly beveled)

27

Outline: 7   **Bangs:** light   **Cuts:** cut 2-back, cut 3-sides

110

Outline: 2-lower Nape   **Bangs:** med.   **Cuts:** 5-front and sides, cut 6 back, cut 3 rest   **Alts:** dovetail neckline

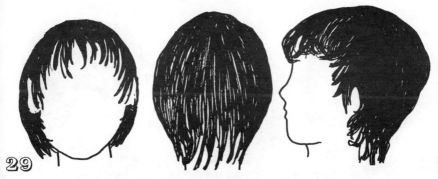

Outline: 7   **Bangs:** medium   **Cuts:** cut 5
Alterations: cut "V" shapes into ends of hair

Outline: 3   **Bangs:** medium   **Cuts:** cut 5
Alts: square neckline, "V" shapes cut into hair ends

111

Outline: 2 **Bangs:** heavy **Cuts:** cut 5
Alterations: square neckline, medium square sideburns

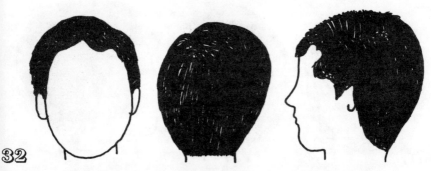

Outline: 1 **Bangs:** medium **Cuts:** cut 5
Alterations: square neckline, medium angled sideburns

Outline: 1 **Bangs:** medium **Cuts:** cut 5
Alterations: oval neckline, medium square sideburns

112

34

Outline: 1 **Bangs:** medium **Cuts:** cut 5
Alterations: round neckline, long square sideburns

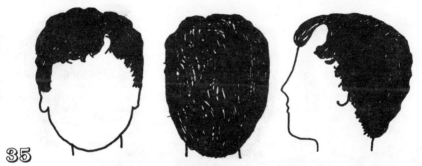

35

Outline: 2 **Bangs:** heavy **Cuts:** cut 5
Alterations: oval neckline, short slanted sideburns

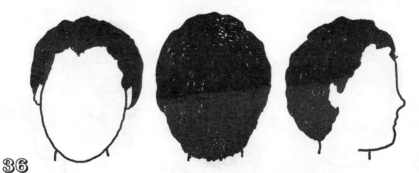

36

Outline: 1 **Bangs:** medium **Cuts:** cut 5
Alterations: round neckline, medium square sideburns

Outline: 3 **Bangs:** none **Cuts:** cut 5
Alterations: oval neckline, long slanted sideburns

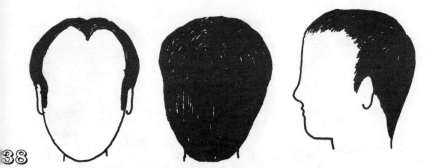

Outline: 1 **Bangs:** medium **Cuts:** cut 5
Alterations: round neckline, long slanted sideburns

Outline: 1 **Bangs:** medium **Cuts:** cut 5
Alterations: square neckline, no sideburns

114

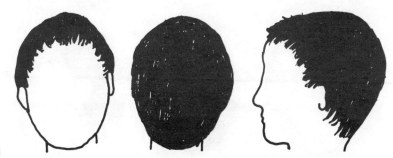

40

Outline: 2   **Bangs:** medium   **Cuts:** cut 5
Alterations: round neckline, short slanted sideburns,
"V" shapes cut into ends of hair

41

Outline: 1   **Bangs:** medium   **Cuts:** cut 6
Alterations: square neckline, medium slanted sideburns, leave length at corners to create square edges

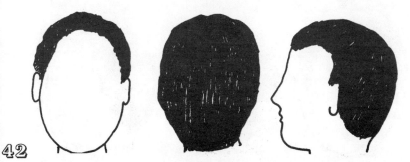

42

Outline: 1   **Bangs:** medium   **Cuts:** cut 6
Alterations: square neckline, short square sideburns

Outline: 1 **Bangs:** medium **Cuts:** cut 6
Alterations: oval neckline, short slanted sideburns

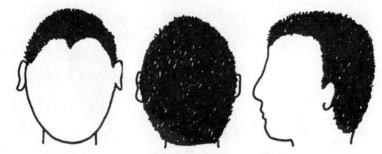

Outline: 1 **Bangs:** medium **Cuts:** cut 6
Alterations: square neckline, medium slanted sideburns

Outline: 1 **Bangs:** none **Cuts:** cut 5
Alterations: square neckline, medium slanted sideburns

116

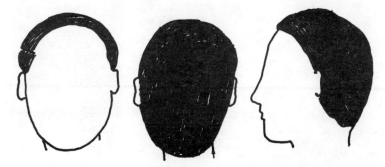

46

Outline: 1   **Bangs:** none   **Cuts:** cut 5
Alterations: round neckline, no sideburns

15

WAYS TO WEAR HAIR

120

121

123

STYLING TIPS

BLOW DRYING

Towel dry as much wetness out of the hair as possible, leaving the hair damp.

Have your client bend forward at the waist. Her head should be tipped completely upside down, letting the hair dangle freely.

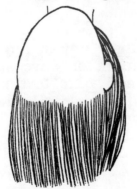

Blow dry your client's hair in this upside down position until the hair is barely damp.

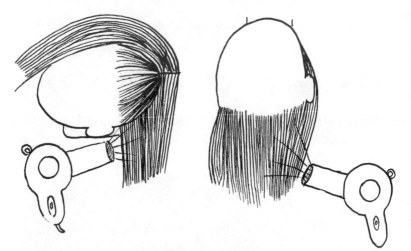

Have your client stand right side up again and part her hair where she desires.

At this point, apply any styling aid such as gel, mousse, lotion, or wave set. This will give body and add extra texture to the hair for a longer holding style. Do this by squeezing a small amount in the palm of your hand. Rub your hands together and distribute it evenly to your client's hair. If your client prefers, the hair may be left natural without any styling aid.

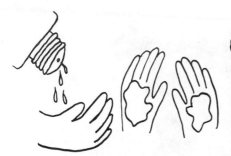

Part your client's hair down the back, dividing it into two sections (one on either side).

Clip these two sections up and out of the way leaving just the bottom third of each section down. (When the underneath hair is dry, it will give the hairstyle more volume, fullness and shape).

Dry the bottom third of the hair, starting at the roots and working toward the ends. Give direction to the hair with a brush or your fingers.

When the bottom third of your client's hair is dry, take the middle third of the hair down from each section. Style it the same way.

When the middle third of your client's hair is dry, take the top third of the hair down from both sections. Style it the same way. Now your style is complete... unless more curl is desired.

Curl Iron

After your client's hair is completely dry a curling iron can be used to enhance the style by adding curl. The curling iron is generally used to curl just the ends, while hot rollers or curlers give curl to the entire hairshaft.

Use the curling iron sparingly. If clamped down on the ends for too long, dryness and damage may result.

Wrap your client's hair around the curling iron, turning it in the direction you want the hair to curl.

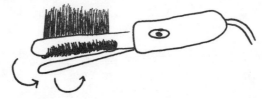

For short hair lay your comb flat against the base of your client's scalp just below the hair being curled. This will protect her scalp from accidentally being touched and burned by the hot iron.

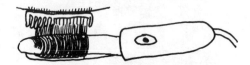

CONCLUSION

Now that you're through, isn't haircutting easier and more fun than you thought it would be? Just because you've reached the end of this book doesn't mean learning ends. Let this be the starting point from which you launch out, casting fears aside and begin to unleash your creative spirit. The only limitation as to what hair style you can create is your own mind. I hope this book has expanded your mind and that haircutting is as enjoyable for you as it is for me.

If this book has helped you to discover a natural talent for cutting hair, I would encourage you to consider beauty school. The professional field of cosmetology offers a variety of careers.

TO ORDER: please fill out the order form
and send to:
Punches Productions
P.O. Box 601477
South Lake Tahoe, CA 95702-1
Or Call 1-(800) 833-8778
or 1-(916) 544-7981 inside California

Name
Address
City   state   zip
Phone (   )

Catalog Number	Description		Qty.	unit Price	Total
1001	How to Simply Cut Hair	**(Book)**		$8.95	_____
1002	Cutting Children's Hair	**(Book)**		7.95	_____
1003	Simply Perm Hair	**(Book)**		6.95	_____
1004	Simply Highlight Hair	**(Book)**		6.95	_____
1005	How to Simply Cut Hair Better (*Advanced Haircutting*)	**(Book)**		9.95	_____
2001	How to Simply Cut Hair	**(Video)**		29.95	_____
2002	Cutting Children's Hair	**(Video)**		29.95	_____
2003	Simply Perm Hair	**(Video)**		19.95	_____
2004	Simply Highlight Hair	**(Video)**		19.95	_____
3001	The Basic Haircutting Kit		_____	29.95	_____
4001	Practice Doll Head		_____	24.95	_____

Calif. residents add 7% sales tax   _____
Shipping charges add **$1.00** per item   _____
Total Cost   _____

All checks payable to **Punches Productions**. Allow up
to 6 weeks for delivery. Money orders will be shipped
immediately upon receipt. **C.O.D.** charges can be paid
for in cash or money order <u>only</u>.

Satisfaction guaranteed.